AARON

ABRAHAM

ADAM

ALTAR

ANGELS

ANNOTATED

ANTICHRIST

APOCRYPHA

APOSTLES

ARCHANGEL

ASCENSION

BAPTISM

BARABBAS

BARTHOLOMEW

BETHLEHEM

BETRAYAL

BIBLE STUDY

BIBLICAL

BONDED LEATHER

BORN AGAIN

BREAKING OF BREAD

CAIN AND ABEL

CANAANITE

CARPENTER

CHAPTER

CHOSEN PEOPLE

CHRISTMAS

CHURCH

COMMENTARIES

COMPUNCTION

CONCORDANCE

CONSECRATE

CONTRITE

CONTRITION

CORINTHIANS

CROSS

CRUCIFIXION

DAVID

DEAD SEA SCROLLS

DEMONS

DEUTERONOMY

DEVIL

EASTER

EDITION

ELOHIM

EPIPHANY

ESAU

ETERNAL LIFE

EVE

EVIL

EXCOMMUNICATE

FAITH

FAMILY BIBLE

FAST

FORGIVENESS

FRANKINCENSE

FREE WILL

GALILEE

GARDEN OF EDEN

GOD

GODS LAW

GODHEAD

GOLIATH

GOLD

GOOD FRIDAY

GOSPEL

GRACE

GUILT

HARDCOVER

HARMONY OF THE GOSPELS

HEAVEN

HEBREW BIBLE

HEBREW

HELL

HEROD

HOLY

HOLY SPIRIT

IMMORTALITY

IMPRINTING

INDEXING

ISHMAEL

JACOB

JAMES

JEHOVAH

JERUSALEM

JESUS

JESUS CHRIST

JOHN

JOHN THE BAPTIST

JOSEPH

JUDAS

JUDEA

JUDGMENT

JUSTIFY

KING JAMES VERSION

KING SAUL

KINGDOM OF GOD

KINGS

LAST SUPPER

LAWS LAZARUS

LENT

LEVITICUS

LOAVES AND FISHES

LUCIFER

LUKE

MAGI

MANS LAW

MANGER

MARK

MARY MAGDALENE

MATTHEW

MESSIAH

MICHAEL

MIRACLES

MOSES

MYRRH

NATIVITY

NEW TESTAMENT

NICENE CREED

OLD TESTAMENT

ORDINATION

ORIGINAL SIN

PARABLE

PAUL

PENANCE

PENITENCE

PENITENT

PENTECOST PETER

PHILISTINE

PHILIP

PONTIUS PILATE

PREDESTINATION

PREMORTAL LIFE

PRIEST

PRIESTHOOD

PROPHECY

PROVIDENCE

PSALM

PURGATORY

QUIET

RAPTURE

REDEEM

REGENERATION

RELIGION

REPENT

REPENTANCE

RESURRECTION

REVELATIONS

SABBATH

SAINT

SAINT JOHN THE BAPTIST

SALVATION

SAMUEL

SANCTIFICATION

SANCTIFY

SATAN

SCRIPTURE

SECOND COMING

SERPENT

SHEPHERDS

SIMON

SIN

SON OF MAN

STABLE

STAR

TEN COMMANDMENTS

THE FALL

THE HOLY TRINITY

THE MESSAGE

THEOLOGY

THOMAS

THREE KINGS

TORAH

TRANSFORMATION

TRANSUBSTANTIATION

TWELVE APOSTLES

UNDERSTAND

VERSE

VIRGIN BIRTH

VIRGIN MARY

WORSHIP

XYLOPHONE

YAWEH

ZEBEDEE

ZEPHANIAH

ZONDERVAN